Kym and Yez Go Riding

By Sally Cowan

The sun was shining when Kym got to the pony club.

Jenny waved at Kym and Dad.

Kym hoped Yez would be happy to see him.

"Do you want to go riding with Yez?" asked Jenny.

"Yes please!" replied Kym.

Kym was excited because he liked Yez the most!

Yez the shy pony was hiding by a bush.

She was busy biting some grapes.

But then Yez saw Kym and raced up to him.

"Hi, Yez!" Kym said, smiling.

Kym stroked Yez's nose.

Yez was excited and happy to see Kym.

Kym changed into his riding top and pants.

He put on his tall riding boots.

He put on his helmet to be safe while he was taking Yez for a ride.

Kym and Yez rode up a sloping track to the top of the hill.

Kym let Yez walk around for a while.

Yez loved grazing on the hill.

Kym was shaking the snack bag to get Yez to come back.

Then Yez swiped a snack from Kym's hand!

They rode back down the hill.

Jenny smiled.

"You are a great rider, Kym!"
she called.
"And you two make the
cutest team!
You should go in a riding event!"

Yez nudged Kym.

CHECKING FOR MEANING

1. How is Yez described in the text? *(Literal)*
2. Where did Yez and Kym go on their ride? *(Literal)*
3. Do you think Yez likes Kym? *(Inferential)*
4. Is it a good idea for Kym and Yez to go in a riding event? Why? *(Evaluative)*

EXTENDING VOCABULARY

hiding	What is the base of the word *hiding*? How does the base change when the *ing* suffix is added?
raced	How would you move if you raced? What is another word the author could have used instead of *raced*?
rider	Look at the word *rider*. What other word in the story has the same base? How is the meaning of *rider* linked with the meaning of the base?

MOVING BEYOND THE TEXT

1. What do you know about ponies? Are they taller than you? What do they eat? Have you ever seen a pony in real life? What did you notice?
2. Kym changed into different clothes for riding. Why do you think he did this? What other kinds of activities or sports require different clothing?
3. Kym is part of a pony club. What other kinds of clubs or teams can kids join? Do you belong to any clubs or teams, or would you like to join any?
4. Would you rather go for a walk or ride a pony? Why?

TIME TO WRITE

Write about what you think happens next in the story. Do Kym and Yez compete in a riding event? What happens at the event?